LALIBELLA THE LADYBUG PAINTS HER WORLD

BY KIA JANEEN SMITH

And do not be conformed to this world, but be transformed by the renewing of your mind, so that you may prove what the will of God is, that which is good and acceptable and perfect.
—Romans 12:2

Copyrights @ 2017 by Kia Janeen Smith
All rights reserved
No part of this publication may be reproduced, stored in a retrieval system, or transmitted in any form or by any means, electronic, mechanical, photocopying, recording, or otherwise without written permission of the publisher.
ISBN 978-0-692-85409-9

To my Dear Son Kekoa

Thank you for helping me create the characters in this story.
Together we are painting our world…….

-Mommy

Once upon a time, in a small valley nestled beneath a Mystical Mountain, lived a village of little red ladybugs, and in this village, was an elderly couple named Mr. and Mrs. Rose.

Year after year the couple worked in their garden sweeping and cleaning all the tiny aphids away. But Mr. and Mrs. Rose grew tired of their day to day life in the garden. There was one thing they wanted more than anything else in the world, and that was to have a little one of their own, yet they had not been so fortunate.

If they truly wanted to have a ladybug child there was one option left; to go to the Mystical Mountain and find the Secret Garden where Kibra "The Great" Lady Dragonfly lived.

They heard stories from the other ladybugs, that if one could find the Secret Garden, then Kibra "The Great" Lady Dragonfly would grant one wish in the ladybug's lifetime.

So, Mr. and Mrs. Rose packed their belongings and went on a quest to find the Secret Garden where they hoped their wish for a little one would finally come true.

As the elderly couple traveled up the winding pathway of the Mystical Mountain, they used their canes as hiking sticks to help them climb up the rocky trails. After their long, exhausting journey, they finally reached the top of the mountain.

"We made it!" Mr. Rose cried joyfully.

"Yes dear, we did…. but I'm so tired," gasped Mrs. Rose.

Just as they caught their breath, they looked up to see a swarm of angry bees headed toward them. Frightened and fearful of the sting, they ran and hid behind a huge crystal rock while holding each other tight. The bees buzzed loudly, as they dipped and dived, flapping their wings furiously before darting off into the distance.

As the bees cleared away, Mr. and Mrs. Rose continued to walk down a narrow pathway that had a glimmering light at the end. When they reached the end, they saw an amazing garden filled with many sparkling flowers. There were roses made of rubies, lilies made of crystal, and daffodils that glowed in the night.

As Mr. and Mrs. Rose entered the Secret Garden, they heard a voice that echoed, "Who has entered my garden?"

"It's Mr. and Mrs. Rose from the village below," Mr. Rose answered in a nervous voice.

"Why have you come to the garden today?" the mysterious voice asked.

Mrs. Rose stepped forward boldly and said, "We've come to wish for a little one of our own to love and cherish.

Suddenly, they felt a light breeze above their heads as Kibra flew out from her hiding place. As they looked up, Kibra gracefully flew closer toward them, opened up her beautiful colored wings and presented a little ladybug child.

"Because you were successful in your journey to find me, I shall grant your wish. Her name is Lalibella!" she said, as she handed the couple their child.

Lalibella was a unique and special ladybug. She had teal eyes that sparkled like the stars in the sky, and her shell glistened like an amethyst gemstone.

"She's beautiful!" said Mrs. Rose. "But why is her shell purple and not red like ours?"

Kibra replied, "I can assure you that you will see her true color in due time."

The happy couple returned home to their small village and raised Lalibella with much love and joy.

As Lalibella grew older, she noticed she was different from the other ladybugs.

"Why is my shell purple and not red like the other ladybugs?" she asked her parents.

"Don't worry, my dear!" said Mrs. Rose, comforting her daughter. "Kibra "The Great" assured us that your true color will show in due time!"

Day after day, and year after year, Lalibella gazed into her mirror to see if the color of her shell had changed to red, but it had not.

Soon Lalibella became frustrated and tried almost everything to change the color of her shell.

She tried rubbing a patch of red strawberries all over herself, only to break out into hives.

As Kibra watched Lalibella from up high in her Secret Garden, she began to sympathize with Lalibella's frustrations. She decided that it was time to help Lalibella embrace the color of her shell.

"I will send my little assistants, Oliver the Aphid and Holly the Social Butterfly, to help Lalibella," Kibra thought to herself.

Oliver and Holly quickly left the Mystical Mountain and headed toward the village to find Lalibella.

One sunny afternoon while Lalibella was sweeping the tiny aphids away, she ran into Oliver the Aphid.

"Oh my! You're big for an aphid!" she screeched. "I'd better get a bigger broom to swat you with."

Holly saw that Oliver was in terrible danger, so she dashed out of the flowers to try to stop Lalibella.

"Please don't swat Oliver!" Holly pleaded. "We are here to help you!"

"I don't believe you!" Lalibella yelled, as she kept on swatting Oliver. The broom narrowly missed the overgrown aphid, as he kept jumping away to avoid Lalibella.

"Take a good look at me Lalibella. Have you ever seen an aphid as handsome as me?" Oliver said charmingly. "I'm unique and different, just like you. Did I mention handsome?"

"Okay, Oliver, I think she gets your point!" Holly chuckled.

"Lalibella, we are from the Secret Garden, just like you," Holly explained. "Kibra 'The Great' sent us here to help you embrace the color of your shell."

Lalibella felt in her heart that Holly was telling the truth. She hesitated for a moment, then put down her broom. From that day forward the unique trio became very close friends.

As the seasons changed from sizzling summers to the whitest winters, Lalibella celebrated her twelfth birthday. Holly and Oliver brought Lalibella a gift from Kibra "The Great." It was a beautiful golden box and inside was a sparkling teal paintbrush exactly the color of her mystical eyes.

Lalibella loved to paint and was eager to start using her new paintbrush, so she went out to the village and painted everything within her imagination. Suddenly, she had an idea that painting her shell red was the solution to all of her worries. Afterwards, she ran out to play with the other ladybugs.

"My true color finally came through!" she proclaimed to the other ladybugs.

But when Oliver saw that Lalibella painted her shell red, he became worried that Kibra would find out. So, he ran to Holly in desperation.

"Holly! Holly! We were sent here to help Lalibella accept the color of her shell — not to paint it red." He sighed. But Holly, being a social butterfly, was having way too much fun with Lalibella and her new friends to pay any mind to what Oliver was saying.

So thereafter, each day before Lalibella went out to play, she painted her purple shell red. But one day, while Lalibella was outside playing with the other ladybugs, it began to rain. As the rain poured heavily, it washed all the paint off Lalibella's shell. Everyone saw that her shell was still purple. Lalibella was so embarrassed. She ran home with tears and raindrops falling down from her cheeks into a puddle of watered down red paint.

As Kibra watched Lalibella from up high in her Secret Garden, she saw things were not going as planned.

"It's time that I take matters into my own hands," she thought. Kibra then decided to go down to the village and transform herself into a ladybug, to disguise as the new substitute teacher at Lalibella's school.

"Hello, class!" she greeted them as she walked into the classroom. "My name is Mrs. Great, and I will be your new substitute teacher." By the end of the school day, the children loved her because she spoke with wisdom and grace.

As time went by, Kibra became very close to Lalibella. She wanted to open her eyes about being unique and different.

"I'm so different from the other ladybugs," Lalibella pouted.

Kibra smiled and replied, "Yes, you are different, but instead of trying to change yourself to fit in with the other ladybugs, maybe you should show them how beautiful it is to be different."

The next day, Lalibella went out to play with the other ladybugs. Each day, she grew more confident in her purple shell. All the ladybugs, including Mr. and Mrs. Rose, began to see there was something special about Lalibella's true color. They all gathered around as they watched Lalibella, "Paint Her World."

"I wish we could all be different colors like in a rainbow," one of the ladybugs shouted with joy.

"Can you paint us all different colors?" another ladybug asked.

Lalibella hesitated for a moment, "Well, I've always imagined what it would be like if we were a village of rainbow colored ladybugs, but instead of paint, I think I have a better idea!"

Using her imagination Lalibella painted a doorway and entered the Secret Garden to find Kibra "The Great" Lady Dragonfly.

As she entered the garden, a voiced echoed, "Who has entered my garden?"

She replied, "It's me, Lalibella."

Kibra flew out to meet Lalibella.

"Hello, my dear Lalibella. Why have you come to my garden today?" Kibra asked.

Lalibella replied, "The other ladybugs wish that we all could be different, just like the colors in a rainbow! Can you grant their wishes?"

"My dear Lalibella, I can only grant one wish to a ladybug who goes through their own journey to find my Secret Garden" Kibra explained.

Lalibella's face fell with disappointment. But Kibra had a softness towards Lalibella, so she flew back and forth as she thought over Lalibella's request.

"However, you did show the others how beautiful it is to be unique and different," Kibra said as she pondered. "Therefore, I will give them each a color that reflects their true color from the inside, just like you were created purple."

"Does this mean I'm purple on the inside?" Lalibella asked

"That is correct!" Kibra replied. "My dear Lalibella, colors have meaning, and your color of purple represents ambition, creativity, and most of all royalty. This is what you represent from the inside and out."

As Kibra spoke, Lalibella felt a great comfort in her heart, because she finally understood the meaning of her true color.

Lalibella then returned to her village back through the doorway of her imagination, and as she arrived, she saw a village of rainbow colored ladybugs, just as she had always imagined.

Painting My World
"The Story behind the Story"

As my mother and I navigated through the terminal at IAH Airport a few years ago, I looked around and it seemed like every little girl was wearing "Hello Kitty." I remember thinking to myself, *"Maybe I should make my own brand for little girls and bring something new and different with meaning to the character."* I started to brainstorm while I was on the plane, but became very anxious and couldn't sit still, so I started to draw what was in my head. I smiled at the sketch after I was done, but my mother was leaning over to see what I drew and said, *"Try giving her some Afro-Puffs."* It seemed weird to me, but I was intrigued, so I took her advice and immediately added afro-puffs to my drawing. The style reminded me of the way my mom used to do my hair as a little girl born in the 70's. Right there on the plane, a special purple ladybug was born.

While thinking of what to name her, my heart led me to the two countries that fascinated me with regards to the history of the royal African families: Egypt and Ethiopia. I was specifically looking for a name that started with an "L" and came across the Ethiopian city, *Lalibela*. I loved how the name sounded and decided to change the spelling to Lalibella, using a "double L" in the name. After I discovered the history of *Lalibela* and its meaning, everything finally came together. I shared my concept for Lalibella with my family & friends and they encouraged me to create friends for her. So, with the help of my son Kekoa, we began to sketch the rest of the characters. As I developed the story, I saw a reflection of my life as a young girl. The tale of a little purple ladybug that went on a journey to self-discovery was definitely a story I could relate to.

Lalibella's story reminded me of the girl I was before moving from the suburbs to the inner-city. I always had a personality full of sunshine with a valley girl accent that I developed from growing up in a suburban environment, so I struggled as I tried to fit in with the inner-city girls and was teased for being different." I went from changing the clothes I wore, to cutting my hair like Salt-N-Pepa, when really, I just wanted to wear lace gloves and fluorescent socks like Cyndi Lauper. Writing the story of Lalibella gave me insight to identify what caused me to lose my shine.

My dream is to share "Lalibella the Ladybug" and her story with the world, to be a shining light, and hopefully help individuals to love their true inner beauty. I believe that everyone should discover their true colors from the inside just like Lalibella does in this story.

Discover it, embrace it, and let it shine!

~**Kia J. Smith**

www.ingramcontent.com/pod-product-compliance
Lightning Source LLC
Chambersburg PA
CBHW041411160426

42811CB00106B/1668